How To Join Mouldings ;

Or,

The Arts Of Mitring and Coping

By

Owen B. Maginnis

1892

A Facsimile Reprint
of an original book from our personal library

Introduction by Gary Roberts

The Toolemera Press

www.toolemera.com

Art Of Mitring :
How To Join Mouldings; Or, The Arts Of Mitring and Coping
by Owen B. Maginnis
New York: William Comstock, 23 Warren St.
1892

International Standard Book Number
ISBN : 978-0-9825329-6-6
(Trade Paperback)

Published by
The Toolemera Press
Dedham, Massachusetts
U.S.A. 02026

http://toolemera.com

Manufactured in the United States of America

Introduction
by Gary Roberts

"There is no carpenter, cabinet-maker, or other artisan, who will not find it a benefit to be thoroughly familiar with the proper methods to follow in joining mouldings together, or as it is technically termed, "mitring" them, etc."

Owen B. Maginnis, 1892

While major texts on architecture, carpentry, joinery and cabinet-making had offered some instructions to the artisan in the laying our and forming of the mitre joint, none had offered an explanation in a manner both readily understood and usable in daily work.

Owen Maginnis saw fit (no pun intended) to write of his practical expertise in the finer points of creating the mitre joint. Clearly stated, thoroughly explained and illustrated by over 40 engravings, *The Art Of Mitring* discusses the practices of mitring versus coping and when to choose either form. The author describes how to determine suitable angles, how to layout cut lines and what tools are best suited to the tasks.

Toolemera Press Facsimile Reprints

The Toolemera Press reprints classic books and ephemera on early tools, trades and industries. We will only reprint items held in our personal library. We will never use a source document from any online document depository. The Toolemera Press manages every aspect of the publishing process. All imaging is accomplished either in-house or by contract with respected document imaging services. We use Print-On-Demand to keep pricing affordable.

http://toolemera.com

PLAN OF A GEOMETRICAL WOODEN CEILING.

Owen B. Maginnis, Designer.

HOW TO JOIN MOULDINGS;

OR,

The Arts of Mitring and Coping.

A complete treatise on the proper modern methods to apply practically in joining mouldings.   A book for working carpenters, joiners, cabinet-makers, picture frame
makers and wood-workers.   Clearly
and simply explained by over
40 engravings, with
full directive
text.

———————

By OWEN B. MAGINNIS,

AUTHOR OF "PRACTICAL CENTRING," "THE CARPENTER'S HANDOOK"
(LONDON), ETC.

———————

NEW YORK:
WILLIAM T. COMSTOCK,
23 WARREN ST.
1892.

INTRODUCTION.

THERE is no carpenter, cabinet-maker, or other artisan, who will not find it a benefit to be thoroughly familiar with the proper methods to follow in joining mouldings together, or, as it is technically termed, "mitring" them, etc. As there has never been any book printed treating at length on this important art, I have carefully prepared this little work, and feel confident that it will be found of great service in and out of the shop, both by practical men and amateurs. The contents are all gathered from practical experience, and can therefore be followed in actual work without any doubt as to their accuracy.

I beg to acknowledge the kindness of the publisher of the *Manufacturer and Builder*, who has permitted me to reproduce the "Art of Coping."

THE AUTHOR.

CONTENTS.

CHAPTER I.

The Definition of a Mitre—Mitre Boxes: How to Make and Lay Them Out...................................... 9–15

CHAPTER II.

Sawing the Mitre Box—Mitring Simple Mouldings and Proving the Cuts in the Mitre Box................. 16–24

CHAPTER III.

Mitring Panel and Raised Mouldings..................... 25–30

CHAPTER IV.

To Mitre on Octagon and Polygonal Figures—The Mitres Formed by Straight Mouldings Intersecting with Circular Mouldings; also Mitres of Circular Mouldings Intersecting..................................... 31–40

CHAPTER V.

Mitring Crown or Sprung Mouldings—Base and Wall Mouldings, or Door Trim......................... 41–48

CHAPTER VI.

Mitring Chair Rail, Picture Moulding, Column Bases, and the Use of the Mitre Templet..................... 49–54

CHAPTER VII.

Varying Mitres in Both Straight and Circular Mouldings.. 55–62

CHAPTER VIII.

A Description of a Combination of Many and Various Mitre Joints, Illustrated by the Frontispiece—A Geometrical Ceiling Design......................... 63–65

CHAPTER IX.

The Art of Coping Mouldings......................... 66–73

CHAPTER I.

"MITRE" is defined architecturally by Webster as the "joint formed by two pieces of moulding each cut at an angle and matching together; to meet and match together on a line bisecting the angle of junction, especially when at a right angle; to cut the ends of two pieces obliquely and join them at an angle."

The above definition of the great lexicographer is really in substance the full definition of the term and the way it is employed, so we will at once proceed to describe the different forms of mitres, from the simplest to the most difficult, giving each in detail and illustrating all methods in full, with the appliances necessary for accurate cutting, etc.

THE MITRE BOX.—This indispensable adjunct for the purpose of cutting mouldings on an angle is well known, yet so important is it that it must be perfectly and

accurately constructed so as to insure the
perfection of the mitre.   Fig. 1 represents
a mitre box as it ought to be made by carpenters in the shops or building, and, as
will be seen, consists simply of three pieces
of wood joined together, the size of the
pieces being as near the following dimen-
sions as possible for ordinary mouldings
up to 3½ inches wide and using a 20 or 22-
inch panel saw.   The length of the box

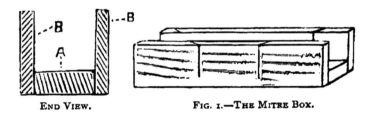

END VIEW.   FIG. 1.—THE MITRE BOX.

should not be less than 18 inches nor more
than 2 feet six inches long.   The bottom
should be 2 inches thick by 4 inches wide
inside so as to insure the sides being firmly
and strongly fastened to its edges; sides,
1¼-inch stuff by 6 inches wide.   Either
pine, oak or soft ash may be used for the
material.   I cannot by any means recommend any of the other woods for this purpose, as they are entirely too subject to at-

mospheric changes. Experience has proven that pine is preferable to any other wood, even though the cuts may wear out sooner through the friction of the saw sideways. If the box be made long enough new cuts can be put in in a few minutes, while the oak box is heavy and unwieldy, though it has the virtues of wearing well.

To construct a mitre box properly the bottom piece, A (see section), must be placed upon the bench and taken out of wind with the fore plane by using straight edges or winding sticks and placing one across each end of the surface to sight across them until they show parallel. If one corner should be higher than the other it must be planed down perfectly level; this being done one edge is straightened with the try-square, after which it is gauged to a parallel width, and the other edge squared. The sides, B B, must also be taken out of wind and one edge straightened. For very good work the sides should also be gauged and planed to a thickness of say 1⅛ inch when 1¼-inch stuff. This planing and gauging must be very well done to gain a perfect box. Before fastening the sides on the bottom they must be carefully gauged with a line 4 inches down on the face side, or on the side which was taken out of wind, which must be done on both sides of the box.   A small wire nail can now be driven close to each end exactly on this line and the side can be placed on the edge of the bottom, keeping the wire nails close down on the face of the bottom, or rather the gauged line fair with the face of the bottom, and the side can be nailed fast to the edges of the bottom, keeping the fastening nails about the centre of the edge.   Should the above work be properly done the inside of the box will measure 4 inches deep, 4 inches wide and be perfectly parallel from end to end, top and bottom at 4 inches, and the sides will stand square to the bottom.   On looking across the top edges of the sides they will be out of wind and show as one. If a box be made in this way it will cut a mitre exactly to a square mitre.

There are two or more ways by which the box can be marked for sawing, but only two which will be accurate. The first consists in taking a drawing board or

clean piece of stuff with a straight edge,
as Fig. 2, and laying off on it a square
whose side is equal to 8 inches, and drawing two diagonals from corner to corner,
as shown, then setting a long bevel to one
of the diagonals and screwing the blade

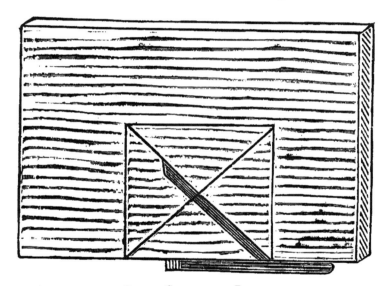

FIG. 2.—SETTING THE BEVEL.

fast in the stock; now take the bevel and
lay it across the edges of the sides of the
box, and, applying it from the outside of
the box, holding the blade firmly down
with the left hand, mark the cut with a
sharp pen-knife on the edge with the right

hand.   Next, reverse the bevel for the left
hand cut, as Fig. 3, and mark it similarly,
which, being done, take the try-square and
square down from the edges on the outside
of the sides to the level of the bottom,
also with a knife, watching that the square
does not move and that the line is perfectly straight.   This is one way to lay out
the cuts.

Another method by which it can be

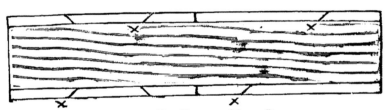

FIG. 3.—TOP VIEW OF MITRE BOX.

done is to take the width of the box inside,
4 inches, and lay it off on the inside arrises of the sides, square, and with the
straight edge and knife, to mark the direction of the angle of 45°, which is now being treated, and square down as before.
I would scarcely recommend that the box
be marked by taking two equal numbers
from the heel of the steel square, because
it is difficult to hold it firmly in position

and there is always the likelihood of the squares being out of true or worn, which will, of course, affect the direction of the cut, though it can be done when the bevel is not available. The reverse cut can either be marked across the right or at the opposite end, but the first has the advantage of leaving the remainder of the box sound for making new cuts when the first ones are worn too wide to be accurate in sawing the moulding.

CHAPTER II.

WHEN the box has been properly marked the next thing to be done is to saw it, or rather to saw into the sides exactly to the knife mark. The saw should not be run down the centre of the mark, but to one side of it, so that the operator may see that it moves down in sawing just to the line. It is therefore best to keep the thickness of the saw blade to the right of the line both across the top edges and on the sides, kerfing both edges simultaneously and reversing the box at intervals to make sure that the saw is not running from the mark, which would throw the cut out of square and spoil the box for good mitring. It is, of course, necessary that the teeth of the saw be sharp and well set and not coarse, so that the cut on the mouldings may be clean enough to obviate planning. Another point I would also strongly recommend is that the saw with which the box is cut, be used in cutting the mitres, because, as it fits best into the kerfs, it will run steadier and more accurately than one which is thinner and has less set. Again, by using a saw with more set the kerfs in the sides are liable to be thrown out of true when placing it in the box. I would decidedly prefer a long saw in preference to a tenon or panel saw, still a 22-inch panel saw is very handy for the box described, as the longer the stroke the better for accurate cutting. Some carpenters prefer to insert a square cut in the box to make butt joints, especially when fixing mouldings in buildings, and it is a judicious and economical practice, when necessary, though, as we are now dealing with the elements of the science, we will proceed with the methods of obtaining ordinary mitres.

Supposing Fig. 4 to be a fillet of wood of any length and it is desired to saw it into such a shape that two or more pieces will be joined at right angles, or square, so as to show a continuous grain and be a close joint, how is it to be done? With the aid of the box just described, very simply. Make the piece long enough to be handily placed in the mitre box, which we will presume is placed upon a bench or table, or even a saw bench, and there fastened by a nail driven diagonally through the ends of the bottom into the bench to

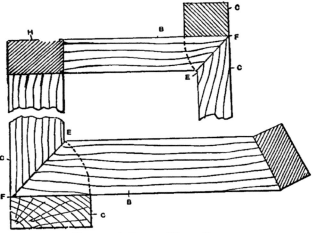

FIG. 4.—A SIMPLE MITRE JOINT.

hold it firmly in one position, then place one piece in the box in the bottom corner against the farthest side, as at A, Fig. 5, and hold it fast there with the thumb of the left hand, the fingers spanning the top edge of the side. Now lift the saw with the right hand, and, inserting it in the kerfs of the box, move it back and forth lightly until it touches the bottom and the end of the mitred piece drops off. We are now presumably making the right hand cut, as B, Fig. 4. Care must be taken to hold the piece immovable in one place until the saw has gone entirely through, as the slightest movement will destroy the shape of the cut and render it inaccurate. The saw will point from left to right in making this

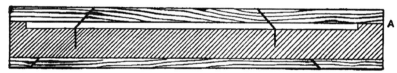

FIG. 5.—TOP VIEW OF BOX WITH SADDLE.

cut, and be placed in the left hand kerfs of the box. To make the left piece that will fit against this, as C, Fig. 4, it will only be necessary to place and hold it in the box as before and saw in the right hand cuts from right to left. When the two are placed together on a level board or surface they will be as represented in Fig. 4, and the mitre joint will be as E F. The inside and outside angles will be 90° and the pieces will be square to each other, giving

a continuous grain on all sides and a perfect, if not invisible, joint on the mitre.
G, Fig. 4, is the section of the mitred ends
which will, of course, be longer than the
cross section of the fillet, H.   The accuracy of the cuts in the box can now be
practically proven by placing the mitred
pieces together and holding them with one
hand or a hand screw while inserting a
true try-square in the angle.   If the stock
and blade of the square touch every part,
then the box is correct ; if not, then the
box is out of true and there is no remedy
but making new exact cuts or kerfs in the
sides, using more care in doing so.   T is
the section of the fillet when sawn at an
octagon, or on the angle of $22\frac{1}{4}$ degrees,
below which is seen the fillet mitred on
the edge and the section of the mitre cut.

The process of mitring, just described,
is applicable to all fillets and simple mould-

FIG. 6.—A QUARTER-ROUND MITRED.

ings. For exam-
ple, the quarter-
round, Fig. 6,
the half-rounds
or beads, Figs.
7 and 8, the round or torus, Figs. 9 and 10,

Fig. 7

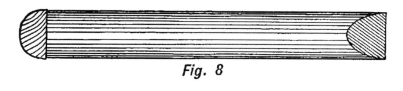

Fig. 8

Fig. 9

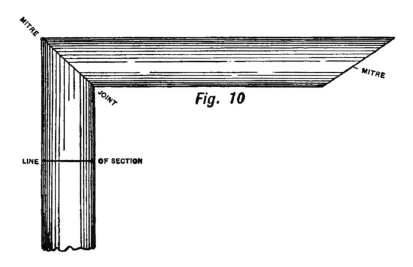

Fig. 10

are all similarly mitred, as are also the "scotias" or "cavettæ," Figs. 11 and 12, which are shown mitred and in projection.

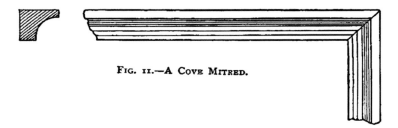

FIG. 11.—A COVE MITRED.

When a fillet or moulding is to be mitred to a fixed length a regular method must be followed to insure its being, when mitred, the exact length required. It is usual to mitre the left hand corner and end first, and then having marked the measurement on the top arris of the piece, as E, to place it in the box, keeping the mark to the side of the saw kerf in the box, because, when it is sawn, the mark must just be on and nothing more. It would leave the piece short by the thickness of the saw blade were this precaution not taken and the mark placed carelessly at the kerf.

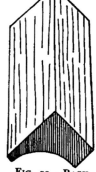

FIG. 12.—BACK VIEW OF COVE.

It will be seen from the above that ex-
treme care is always requisite for proper
mitring, in order that the beveled ends
formed by sawing in the box may fit to
form the angle required *without planing*,
which is rarely done neatly enough to
make a close joint and causes much waste
of time.

A good mechanic will never plane his
mitres, but saw them so accurately that
they will fit to a hair when placed together.

FIG 13.

Fig. 13 shows the right hand mitre of
a compound raised moulding mitred in the
box, A being its cross section and B its
mitred section. In order to acquire practice I would advise a beginner to mitre
four pieces of wood, fillets, or mouldings,
like Fig. 4, together, forming a picture
frame, as it were. This can be done by
first mitring them, say, two 8″ and two
12″ long, and tacking each one as it is
mitred round on a flat board till they

form a border or frame and the joints
come close. There are many who claim
that it is impossible to cut four pieces or
eight mitres so precisely as to fit all round.
This is a fallacy, and after doing it several
times the beginner will see that if his mitre
box be true they will all fit and the frame

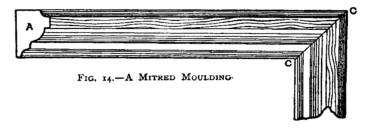

FIG. 14.—A MITRED MOULDING.

will be square. The latter he can determine either by placing a rod across from
corner to corner inside till the diagonals
are equal, or by the method before described with the try-square. Fig. 14 is a
panel mould mitred for a picture frame,
A being the cross section and C C the
joint of the mitre.

CHAPTER III.

MITRING PANEL AND RAISED MOULDINGS.

HAVING considered the simplest form of the science, I will now describe how a raised or rebated moulding can be inserted in a

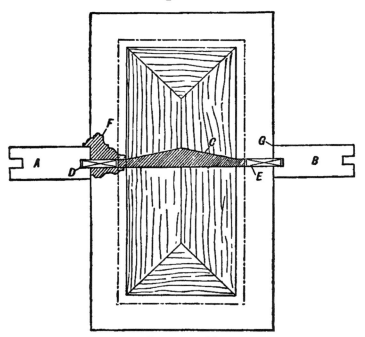

FIG. 15.—PANEL AND MOULDINGS.

panel. Supposing the panel at Fig. 15 to be a panel in a door of any kind, either for a

room or wardrobe, A B being the section
showing the two stiles of the frame A and
B, C the panel, D E the fillets and F the
panel moulding, which has to be mitred
round the inside edges of the frame and
to cover the joint at the arrises, as G, by
the rebate or lips on the moulding F.

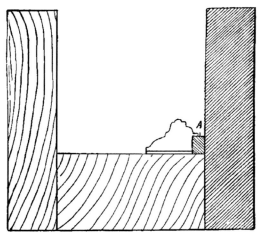

FIG. 16.—BOX WITH SADDLE.

Should the frame be so carefully made and
planed off that the sinkage of the panel
be equal all around, then all that is necessary is to make a saddle as A, Fig. 16,
equal in width to the depth of the sinkage,
which is here $\frac{1}{2}''$, about $\frac{1}{4}$ or $\frac{3}{8}''$ thick, and
place it in the mitre box in the position

shown in the drawing, so that the lips of
the moulding may rest upon it. Fig. 5,
being a plan of the box, illustrates this
more clearly, also how the marks for de-
termining the length are scratched with a
knife on the bottom by squaring out from
the mitre point where the saw intersects it.
Should there be any difference in the sinkage between each corner or angle, then a
saddle, the width of which is equal to the
neat depth, must be used when cutting
the mitres at each individual corner.   This
must be strictly adhered to when there is
a marked difference in order to make the
mitres fit closely, the rebate to come closely
down to a joint on the frame and the inside edge of the moulding close down on
the panel, thereby making a good job.
When the latter is being done the best
method to follow is to place the pieces
round in the panel, just feeling, making
the profiles of the moulding intersect
equally, commencing at the left and working round, and when the four are in to tap
them gently down, using a block, so as
not to bruise the moulding, and a hammer,

making sure that they all fit snugly in
their places.

The usual way to mark the length of
this description of rebated moulding is to
place it in the sinkage of the frame, keeping the left hand mitred end closely into
the corner, and then mark-
ing it with a pocket knife.
This mark is placed to the
square line at Fig. 5 in the
mitre box and when it is
sawn it will be just the
exact length required.

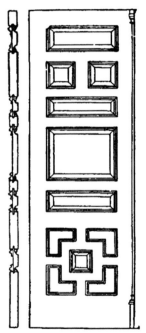

The front door illus-
trated in Fig. 17 has both
flush and raised panels,
but a raised inch moulding
on one, the face side, and
a common o-gee chamfer
moulding on the other.
The full size section, Fig.
18, gives the full profile of

FIG. 17.—DOOR WITH
RAISED MOULDINGS.

each. This door is a very
good example of mould-
ings cut in the way I have just described,
with the addition of having a central
panel with ⌞ panels grouped around,

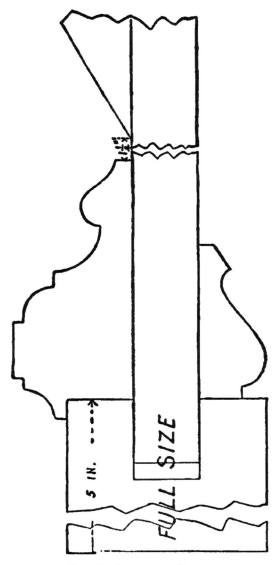

FIG. 18.— SECTION OF FIG. 17.

which gives four outside mitres.   Here the difference between outside and inside mitres must be explained.   An inside mitre is one in which the profile of the moulding is contained, or the outside line and highest part is contained within the angle, and an outside mitre is one which is directly its opposite, or the whole of the moulding is cut round outside the angle. The mitres are similarly sawn in the box, with the exception that the direction of the cut is changed, and instead of being an inside angle the profiles of the moulding intersect on an outside, as shown on the door.   As it often happens from faulty construction that the rails and stiles of a door are slightly out of square, it is advisable to place a try or set square over or in the angles, to make sure that they are correct, or the mitres will show an open joint according as they vary.   When this is the case the best way is to place a thin shaving or strip of cardboard, when mitring, behind one end. of the moulding to make it vary likewise to suit the framing.

CHAPTER IV.

TO MITRE ON OCTAGON AND POLYGONAL
FIGURES.—THE MITRES FORMED BY
STRAIGHT MOULDINGS INTERSECTING
WITH CIRCULAR MOULDINGS, ALSO
MITRES OF CIRCULAR
MOULDINGS INTER-
SECTING.

THE moulding should also be carefully
examined to see that it is stuck the full
thickness, that the rebate is square and
fully fit for the purpose for which it is intended, and it is best to plane the back off
a little on a bevel so that it will fit easily
into its place and tighten as it goes down.
When the moulding is too thick for the
sinkage then it must be backed off until
the distance from the lips to the bottom is
slightly less than the depth from the face
of the frame to the fillet or panel. Ma-
chine-made mouldings often vary in their
outline and thickness, and the operator
will find that when the pieces are driven

into their places one piece may rise over
its fellow and require trimming off to
make the joint exact and the profiles of
the members continuous. As just stated,
when the character of the work is high,
as in cabinet work or the construction of
hardwood finish for or in buildings, it is
best to take precautions to prevent the
occurrence of faults which will necessitate
remedies likely to mar the finished appear-
ance of the workmanship.

Concerning the subject of mitring on
all other angles besides that of 45°, it is to
be said that for this purpose the mitre box
is also requisite, the method of kerfing for
the octagon cut being similar excepting
that the direction of the cut across the box
is only $22\frac{1}{2}$° instead of 45°. All octagons
on different designs are of different sizes,
and a fixed method should be followed
for this and all other sided figures to
determine the direction of the line which
will exactly bisect the angle formed by
the junction of the sides, or, technically
speaking, the mitre. In Fig. 19 the
methods of finding this line will be seen,

embracing the pentagon or five-sided

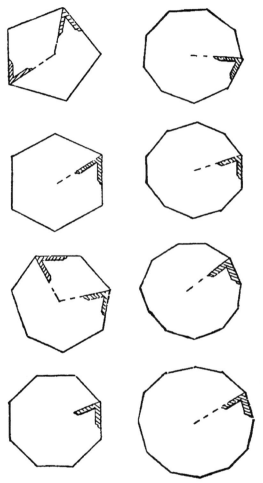

FIG 19.—POLYGONAL FIGURES.

figure, the hexagon or six-sided, the hep-
tagon or seven-sided, the octagon or eight-

sided, the enneagon or nine-sided, the decagon or ten-sided, the undecagon or eleven-sided and the dodecagon or twelve-sided. Therefore, all that is required to find the angles by which the box must be marked for the mitre is to set a bevel to the lines laid down as here shown and to the size desired and to line across the box for the kerfs.

Fig. 20 shows a moulding mitred together on the outside and inside cuts of an octagon, also the mitre of a straight piece with a piece on the octagonal cut of 22½°, which often occurs in practical joinery and demands care in making. In connection with this it might be mentioned that a very simple method to find the bi-section or mitre of any angle is shown at Fig. 20a, which consists of taking any two points equi-distant from the apex of the angle, as A and B, and with a pair of compasses, set to any radius, to strike two intersecting arcs. By joining the points of intersection with the apex by a line, this line will be the exact mitre. This method can be applied here with perfect

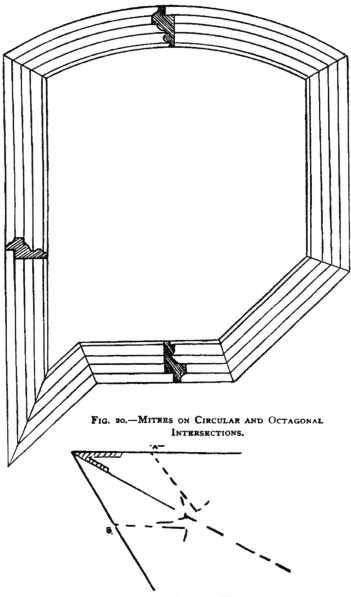

FIG. 20.—MITRES ON CIRCULAR AND OCTAGONAL
INTERSECTIONS.

FIG 20a.—TO FIND ANY MITRE.

success.   At the opposite end of Fig. 20
is illustrated the mitring of a straight
piece of moulding with a curved or circular piece.   As the moulding embraces a
part or arc of a circle, it follows that, being cut by the circle inside the circumfer-
ence, the mitre will be a straight cut.

The feature noticed is amply illustrated
in Fig. 21, which is the junction of a circular and straight moulding, the straight
piece being tangent to the circular and
each having similar members they mitre
perfectly and show good workmanship.
This sketch also shows the joint of a circular moulding with a straight one when
the sweep is a semi-circle, and the sections, as drawn, will give the reader
a clearer explanation of the manner in
which the various members lapse into each
other in passing.   The writer considers
this subject of circles in mitre of so much
importance in the construction of decora-
tive joinery that he would strongly recommend all those interested to closely ex-
amine and study all existing examples of
work already executed.   It is capable of

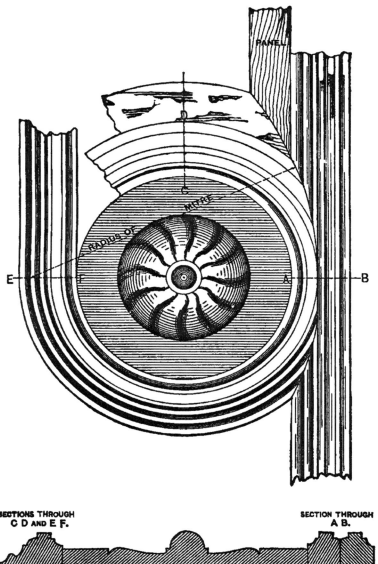

PANEL

SECTIONS THROUGH
C D AND E F.

SECTION THROUGH
A B.

FIG. 21.—CIRCULAR AND STRAIGHT MOULDINGS.

much variation, involving very careful
study in working out in practice.

Fig. 21a is the mitre formed by tangent
circles, which is also a curve.   In connection with this subject it must always be remembered that all curved
mouldings should be turned to a like profile to intersect properly.   This I show at
the section on the line of the mitre.

The drawing, Fig. 22, gives the reader

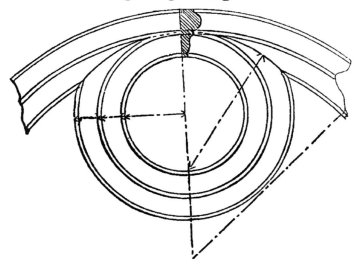

FIG. 21a.—MITRE FORMED BY CONCENTRIC MOULDINGS.

a description of how two circular contiguous mouldings of the same radius and
profiles must necessarily form a mitre

whose direction will be a straight line, but if two circles intersect which are contiguous and radii of different lengths, then the mitre joint will be a curve.

By referring to the geometrical design for a ceiling, Fig. 23, the student will see

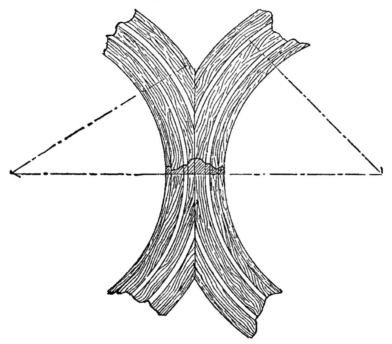

FIG. 22.—MITRE OF TWO ECCENTRIC MOULDINGS.

another and more advanced feature, namely, in the mitring of a straight moulding into one whose peripheral is a

circle, the direction of the straight one being through the diameter, which makes a
straight joint when mitring, also another

FIG. 23.—A MITRED CEILING.

circle cut toward the centre by another
which does not pass to it at right angles
but on an acute angle.

CHAPTER V.

CONCERNING the subject of mitring crown mouldings I would state that there is only one way to mitre a sprung moulding properly, whether it be a crown mould or any kind, and that is to place it in the mitre box against the further side with the side that is to stand perpendicular as on the side of the wall. The two most common kinds of mitre cuts usually made on crown moulds are those on the inside and outside mitres, as A and B, Fig. 24, where the mitred pieces are shown as they will appear from above. When a piece has to be cut on an outside mitre, as on the corner of a building, it is mitred from the corner, or as B, Fig. 24; that is, the direction of the cut will be outside the right angle made by the building; but if it be an inside mitre the mitre joint will be con-

tained within the angle of the building
and it will bisect it.   It is to be said, how-

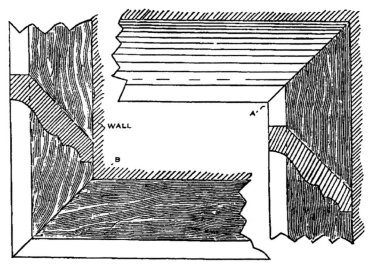

FIG. 24.—A CROWN MOULD MITRED.

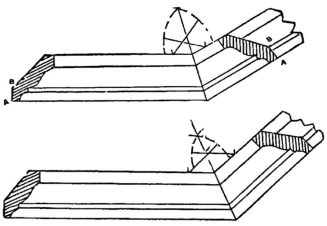

FIG. 25.—HOW TO FIND THE INTERSECTION.

ever, that inside angles, like A, are usually coped, and the method of doing this will be explained hereafter.   Fig. 25 illustrates the manner of mitring a level moulding with one on the pitch on the same surface. Some carpenters maintain that the same conditions prevail here as in the case of a moulding on a pediment mitring and with one on a level, namely, that they won't intersect.   This is an error, as the sketch clearly proves, because each moulding has the same profile, and the only thing essential to insure a perfect intersection is to determine the exact line of the mitre.   It can be done as shown by taking any two points and striking arcs cutting each other, and the point of section being joined with the apex of the angle will give the direction of the mitre joint.   As it often happens that there may be only one gable or pediment on a building, or two of a different pitch, it would scarcely be necessary to make a box for the four or eight cuts, and a very rapid and simple way which I have found to work well is to lay out the direction of the cut on the plumb side which nails against the wall or fascia and square across the bottom edge.

A carpenter with a well filed saw and steady hand can cut this joint clean and straight from the back. Another way which some prefer is to lay the running directions of the moulding out on a board and set each piece up on the laid out lines, then to place the moulding to the lines and square up with a try-square from the line of the mitre as laid out. This method saves more time than by making a box.

To prove that the angle does not regulate and alter the intersection I illustrate at Fig. 26 a large 5-inch crown moulding of ten members which will intersect and be continuous, each to each, provided the profiles run on each piece in the sticker and be entirely alike. I find from experience that by reason of the peculiarity of some stickers there is a variance of some mouldings, and it is therefore wise in the carpenter to measure each piece carefully to insure their intersection and save time in trimming them off to a like profile.

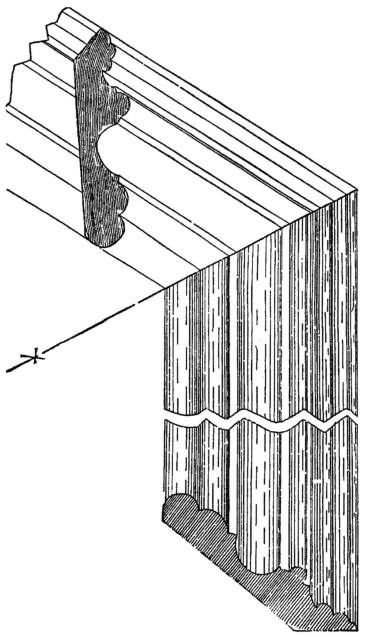

FIG. 26.—LEVEL AND PITCHED MOULDING.

This is rarely done neatly enough to make a clean job because it is necessary to trim as far back as 8 or 9 inches from the mitre to prevent each member appearing round.

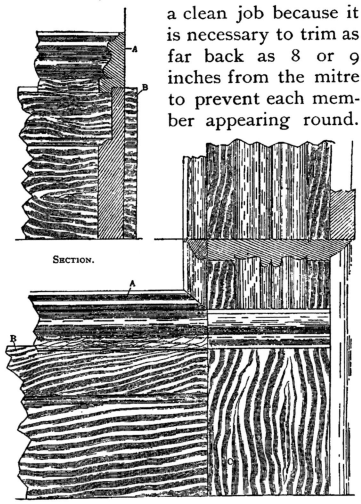

SECTION.

FIG. 27.—A BASE MOULDING AND CASING.

Regarding the mitring of sprung mould-

ings on a curve much the same conditions
prevail as with those stuck flat, but should
the reader desire to become thoroughly
acquainted with this subject I would
refer him to some of the very excellent
works written by various authors treating
on it. There is very little occasion for
this class of work at present, and, even
were it so, I should still refrain from taking and accrediting to myself those ideas
which have been so clearly explained and
illustrated before.

Fig. 27 will explain how the mitring
on door trimming is usually done. A is
the base moulding or top member of the
base. As will be noticed it has three
principal members, comprising the square
or flat surface on the bottom, the main
o-gee and the upper compound moulding.
When the base mould, A, is fitted against
the trim and base block, C, the two bottom members are cut square in the mitre
box, and the top member is mitred to per-
mit the wall moulding (which is really
the top member, to run in separate
lengths) to mitre. It is used for the pur-

pose of covering the joint likely to open between the back side of the door casing and the wall plaster

CHAPTER VI.

MITRING CHAIR RAIL, PICTURE MOULDING.
COLUMN BASES AND THE USE OF
THE MITRE TEMPLET.

FIGURE 28 shows the reader an elevation
and section of a piece of chair rail mitred

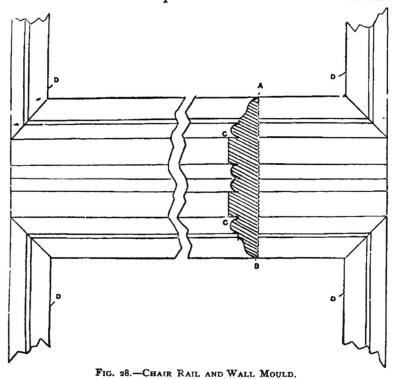

FIG. 28.—CHAIR RAIL AND WALL MOULD.

into the wall mould of a door or window
trim.   A B is the section of the mouldings,
and it will be noticed that the two upper
members, C A and C B, though they are
stuck solid on and form part of the chair
rail, are of the same profile and mitre with
facility with the wall moulding, L.   In
many sections of the country this style of
finish is not used, but in some of the East-

FIG. 29.—PICTURE MOULD.

ern States and in New York City it is the
usual method, and has, I think, many
good qualities which would recommend its
adoption.

The picture mould shown in the drawing, Fig. 29, where it is represented as
being nailed on a wall on which the wall
paper has been pasted, conveys to the

reader the way in which this moulding is placed beneath the frieze. This moulding usually is cut on square inside and outside angles. There is very little to be said explanatory of how it should be mitred, excepting that when gilt moulding is being mitred a very fine tooth saw should be employed in order to avoid breaking the plaster of Paris composition which covers the profiles of the members. Another thing is that the inside angle should never be coped but should invariably be mitred, for the reason that it is almost impossible to cope it with the pen-knife without injuring the gilding.

Fig. 30 represents the mitring of a base moulding round a column whose plan or section is a hexagon. It will be noticed that the base is composed of nothing more than a large moulding stuck in the machine to the design shown in the sketch. Readers will understand for the accurate mitring of such a moulding as this it would be best to construct a special mitre-box, and, after setting a bevel to the angle desired, so mark the box from it and

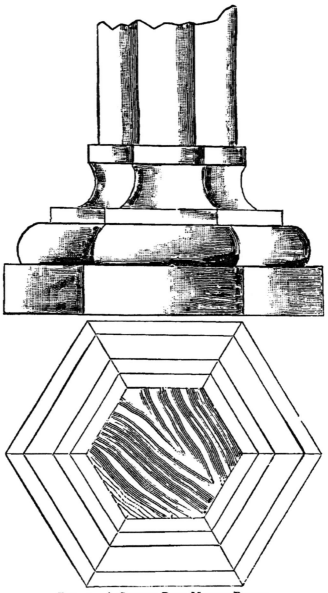

FIG. 30.—A COLUMN BASE MITRED ROUND.

thus insure the accuracy of the length of
each piece.   Nail or glue on each side of
the hexagonal piece.   I would here like to
impress one thing on all readers, and that
is the necessity of making sure that wide
mouldings are straight or even a little hollow on the back side.   This is necessary
when the pieces are affixed to surfaces, and

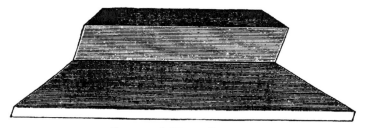

FIG. 31.—A MITRE TEMPLET.

a good plan to follow is to place the edge
of a blade of a try-square across the back,
and, if it be rounding, to plane it to a
slightly hollow surface with a smoothing
plane.

Fig. 31 represents what is commonly
called by carpenters a mitre templet, and
it is used for the purpose of marking all
small mouldings, as beads, quarter-round,
etc.

Fig. 32 shows its application to a quarter-round. The introduction of mitre squares, bevel squares and other modern tools have rendered the use of this instrument more

FIG. 32.

or less obsolete, but the older mechanics regard it as essential in their tool chest and use it largely in putting together beaded framing or other work where small mouldings are to be mitred.

CHAPTER VII.

VARYING MITRES IN BOTH STRAIGHT AND CIRCULAR MOULDINGS.

IN THE ordinary routine of work pertaining to each of the different wood-working crafts, there are certain forms of joints, cuts or important details of construction and decoration which are well known and occur almost daily, and other forms of the same which are varying. As those which are most in use are more easily worked and familiar to the operator, so it must of necessity follow that unusual forms will call forth more labor of brain and manual skill to effect their successful completion. This is particularly applicable in the case of the mitre joint, which every wood-worker is in daily contact with. It is being continually employed in different parts of joinery, in all places where a continuous grain or moulding is required, but the most difficult of all its employments to execute is the mitring of mouldings, both flushed and raised, in framing. Here the intersection of the profile, especially those with many members, necessitates great care in marking the mitre box and sawing it, marking and sawing the moulding, and insuring its perfect intersection before driving the pieces to their permanent place in the panel. Concerning a simple square mitre of the angle of 45°, as it is too well known to require special comment here, we will avoid its consideration, except to recommend readers to take careful heed of three important points, essential to perfect mitring :

First—To mark the mitre box by a bevel set to the diagonal of a square about four inches wide, laid down with a knife on a clean board.

Second.—To mark the box also with the knife and saw, carefully, keeping the saw kerf to one side of the knife mark.

Third.—Saw moulding exactly to the mark made on the panel, and out of one continuous piece for each panel, round the sides, and intersect perfectly before driving down.

Care and exactness will help to perfection and save trimming off afterward.

Fig. 33 represents a piece of ash paneling designed to stand under a stair string.

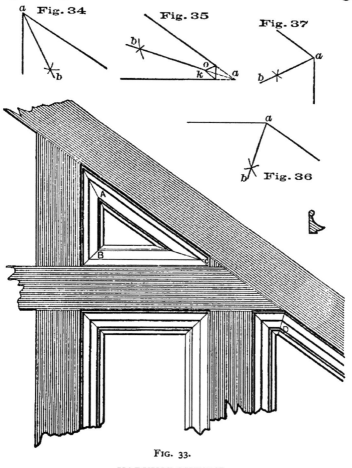

FIG. 33.

VARYING MITRES.

To find the mitre at A, strike out the angle inside the framing at A, like Fig. 34. Take any two points equi-distant from A, the apex of the angle. With the compasses strike the crossed lines shown and draw a line joining their crossing with the apex of the angle. This line will be the exact mitre, and if a level be set to it and marked on a good box, the cut can be got direct from the saw. Fig. 35 shows the compound mitre at C. It is rendered compound by the insertion of a small piece necessary to continue up the mullion below the rail show, and the mitres are found thus : The angle at the corner of the rail and raked piece, being even less than at A, B, will be longer, and this line is gained by the method used above. B being a right angle, the mitre for it is cut in an ordinary 45° box, but C must be cut differently, as its length renders it unhandy for a box. It is recommended that the moulding be marked on the bottom side and the mitre cut square to the bottom to insure a close joint above. This method will always be found suitable for very long cuts. The fifth mitre, shown in Fig. 33 at D, is obtained by the same process as before, and, being short, can be marked on Fig. 36 and cut in the mitre box. Experience has taught that the only way to obtain a perfect mitre is from the saw alone, as it is invariably the case, no matter how carefully the block plane is used, the joint can never be evenly surfaced or satisfaction gained.

Fig. 38 is a diagram of an opening for a panel in a partition or door, etc., showing two methods of ornamenting the angles. The cross sections of the mouldings X[4] are similar, but the shape of the opening would vary according to the arc used, whether internal or external. The circular mouldings B B C are similar, and are of the same section as the straight portions, but A is expanded to conform to the conditions laid down in the plan—*i.e.*, that all the intersections shall be at a true mitre (45°). B B joins the straight parts with a butt joint, C is the same section, and would intersect in the same manner as B if it were in that position; but, following the

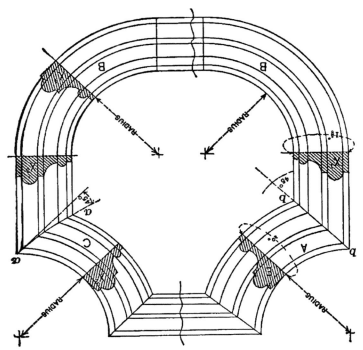

FIG. 38.—DOOR PANEL.

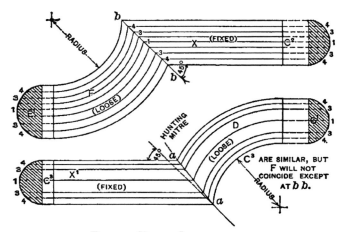

FIG. 39.—VARIED INTERSECTIONS.

plan, it will be seen that it intersects not a true mitre.   But the joint is not a right line, and it is impossible to make the joint in the ordinary manner—*i.e.*, with the saw and plane (for woodwork).   This joint is sometimes called a "hunting mitre," and it must be carved to its true shape.   It will be noticed that it is formed of a pair of curves.   This will perhaps be clearer from an inspection of Fig. 39, and to those interested in the subject (and it is a practical one) if they construct a model from that plan a curious result will be seen.

X, X' are straight lengths of mouldings (any section—in this case semi-circular for simplicity); but the principle can be seen better if a good half-round moulding be selected.

D is a quadrant of a circle, section as X, X', joined so that the marginal lines intersect.   The form of the curved joint *a a* is found by a series of straight and curved auxiliary planes parallel to the axes of D and X'.

F is an arc similar to D internally which intersects X at *b b* at an angle of 45°.   The result is that the point where the angular line cuts the horizontal line is the position where the arc must join the straight line, therefore F is expanded; its true section is shown at E'.

This explains why many workers cannot get a turned moulding and a straight one to intersect at a true mitre, when both are similar in cross section.   When the model is made, alternate the positions of D and F with X and X'.

CHAPTER VIII.

THE ceiling decorated in this manner
would be of the kind technically termed
"planted," or the design of hardwood
planted or nailed on a wooden ground or
smooth ceiling surface, which would be
covered with a prepared cloth capable of
taking paint. The panels are, therefore,
the paneled surface, and the outline of
the design or woodwork.

We will suppose then that the whole
area has the canvas or cloth tacked on and
that it has been given a coat of size to
render it capable of receiving the paint.
It is desired to work out the design in
wood ; how shall it be done ?

First, the design must be detailed ; that

is to say, the main features of the construction will require to be drawn to a large scale or the actual constructed size, so that each part may be distinctly comprehended by the wood-worker and carpenter.

A very simple detail will be necessary here, and merely a section will be needed.

All mitres are simply intersections, and the mitre joint proper is the line of direction which the several and separate members form in blending into each other, each to each, in maintaining their continuity. It will then be clearly seen that if the operator place the pieces, be they either one straight or one curved piece, two curved pieces crossing or intersecting either in a tangential or eccentrical direction, or two straight pieces placed at any angle, the direction of the mitre-line or "joint" will be easily found by laying down the lines which indicate the several members.

Thus it will be readily comprehended that the main lines which form the whole geometrical part of the ceiling are the lines which indicate the members of the mouldings, and all that it will be necessary to do to determine the line of direction of the mitre joint will be to place each moulding where it belongs and mark the intersections. There are fifteen different mitres illustrated in this design, and I think I would be justified in saying that if any practical readers will go to the trouble of making a scale model, they will receive a practical lesson in the art of mitring which will give them the power to obtain any possible mitre on flat surfaces.

CHAPTER IX.

ONE of the means employed by cabinet-makers and carpenters in making joints in r'entrant angles is the art of coping.

The verb "to cope" is used in contra-distinction to "to mitre," a method entirely used for joining pieces of joinery of a con-tinuous grain on exterior angles. Webster gives the word as, to cover; to match against; a covering. So it is admirably adapted, and very appropriate, as when an operator copes, he really covers and matches against.

Coping is principally used for mould-ings, square and flat surfaces being fitted together, one piece abutting against the other; but curved or moulded surfaces can only be coped to a successful inside joint.

Mitring interior angles is very faulty, and is rarely done by mechanics of ability, on account of the liability of one or the

other joint slipping past its fellow, breaking the intersection, and showing end
wood, added to the difference of the profiles of mill-run mouldings. Against
plaster the inside mitre is useless, as one
piece is almost certain to draw and open
the joint when nailing into the studding.
The best way, then, to make this joint is
to cope it.

Fig. 40 represents
a very simple cope,
being a common
shelf cleat, coped
at right angles
against another.
As will be seen, it
is the end cut to
the profile of the
moulding, or bevel,
of the cleat, so that

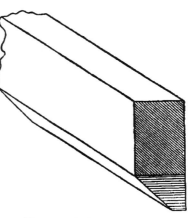

FIG. 40.—A COPED CLEAT.

it will fit tight against it and look as if
mitred.

In order to gain this joint, the piece is
first placed in a mitre box and cut on the
mitre on the side to which the joint fits;
in this case, the right hand. The dotted

line denotes the line of the cut. When this is done, the piece is cut through at an angle, slightly under, so that the joint may touch in every point on the face. When placed in position, if the piece be cut slightly long, the joint will come perfectly close and fit well; but the piece coped to must always be nailed well back and solid before marking the piece to be coped, as it

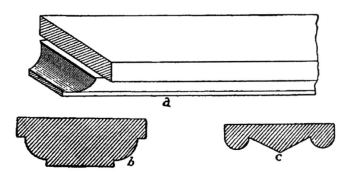

FIG. 42.—MOULDED STRIP COPED.

is certain to yield to the concussion of the hammer. This is a vertical, or plumb, cope.

A horizontal cope is drawn at Fig. 42 and shows a ceiling strip or piece of astragal coped to an ovolo, or rule-jointed edge; *a* is the coped end, done by placing the entire moulding on its back in the mitre-box and mitring each moulding on each side square across the piece, and afterward sawing or chiseling the end out to the profiles made by the saw in mitring, until it appears as in the sketch *a*, and will fit closely against the section at *b*. This cope ought to be slightly hollow, so as to press against the surface of the moulding on the arms of the cope.

The moulding shown at Fig. 42, *c*, cannot be coped, as some of its members are incapable of being so, or sink below others. This will be seen at a glance and the moulding mitred.

It is only in mouldings of this kind where the art cannot be profitably applied; but interior mitres (if they must be used) should be nailed and glued together before setting in position.

When it is found necessary to cope an architrave moulding, like Fig. 43 (a series of compound curves and squares), the mitre box is again brought into requisition and the end brought to the mitred line, always beveling it slightly under, to bring the cope close on the line of A B.

A sharp penknife is essential for good coping, to cut away the wood on the curves exactly to the mitred line, something which can scarcely be done correctly with the compass saw, gouge or chisel, as in soft wood the arris is very liable to break under the pressure of the hand, even

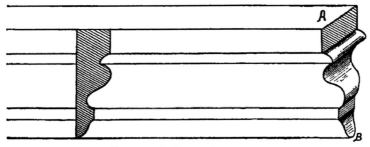

FIG. 43.—A COPED ARCHITRAVE.

though the edge be keen, whereas the small blade of a good pocket-knife, if reasonably sharp, can be very handily swept around the quick curves, and will also cut obliquely against the grain without injuring the edge of the end wood, the grain of which is often short and fragile.

A difficult cope is drawn at Fig. 44, being a section of rebated wainscot capping,
with its wall moulding and another piece
coped to it in a r'entrant corner, at right
angles, left hand. The capping is mitred
in the left hand cut in the box, and then
sawn out close to the mitred line with a
compass saw, and afterward being neatly

FIG. 44.—COPED WAINSCOT CAPPING.

pared exactly to the line, in order that the
joint may show one line. The wall moulding is similarly treated ; but for all mouldings when coping, pieces of the same
thickness and profile ought to be selected.

Obtuse angles might also be coped,
taking care that the end is beveled well
enough to clear the piece running behind
it, otherwise the joint will be *hard* on the

back and open; acute angles will cope easily.

Coping obtuse angles gives a splendid chance to bring the joint close by nailing through the cope into the piece behind, something which can never be done with an inside mitre.

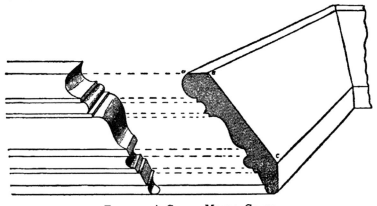

FIG. 45.—A CROWN MOULD COPED.

The crown mould is also fitted by this method when it is returned on inside corners, as on wardrobes, cases, an angle in a house cornice, etc., mitring as before, by placing the length of mould in the box upside down, the part that stands plumb, as *e c* in Fig. 45, against the side of the box, the level part, or cope *d e*, resting flat on the bottom. When cut to an inside mitre, the end is *coped*, or cut out, to cover over the profile *d b*, the coping being all level, or parallel, to *d e*, in the manner represented in the perspective sketch.

Coping on the angle, as on a gable with an eave moulding, can also be done, but the pieces must be wrought so that they will intersect, and continue true—member with member.

In conclusion, it may be said that the system is universal in its use in modern joinery for chair rail, picture mould, crown mould, base necking, wall members, etc., and is very popular among wood-workers, as they cannot, like plasterers, mitre their pieces and then close the joint with putty. It is a rapid, certain and accurate system, and when properly done, especially in the hard woods, produces a good mechanical job.

CPSIA information can be obtained at www.ICGtesting.com
Printed in the USA
LVOW13s0631271113

362925LV00001B/56/P